The Sheep Book

The Sheep Book

Dorothy Hinshaw Patent

Photographs by William Muñoz

DODD, MEAD & COMPANY

New York

Acknowledgments

The author and photographer wish to thank the following for their time and for allowing their sheep or themselves to be photographed for this book: Baron Woolen Mills, page 54; Judy Bell, 76; Leslie Blanding, 56; Gary Boss, 26; Jim Clairmont, 74; Bob Cordis, 51, 53; Nancy Deschamps, 14, 15, 40, 52, 58; Arlo Ellison, 8, 17, 35, 62; Val Geissler, 19, 63; R. J. Harward, 44-46, 65, 67, 68, 70; Bill and Dorothy Judah, 1, 2, 27, 32, 39, 69, 75; Louise Knight, 48, 72; Richard and Shelley Knight, 21, 43; Chester Muñoz, 49; Peggy Muñoz, 55, 57; Cheri Olson, 18; Diane Olson, 16; Ingrid Painter, 28, 77, 78; Sissy Penrod, 64; Richard Race, 20; Sieben Ranch, 10-13, 24, 29-31, 33-34, 36-38, 41, 73, 79; Three Sisters' Southdowns, 42; Ann Trimble, 26, 71; Ralph Wilkinson, 39; Bob Zimmerman, 61, 66. Our thanks also to Thomas Crane and Jill Lane.

Photograph on page 58 is by the author.

1   2   3   4   5   6   7   8   9   10

Library of Congress Cataloging in Publication Data

Patent, Dorothy Hinshaw.
  The sheep book.

  Includes index.
  1. Sheep—Juvenile literature.   I. Muñoz, William.
II. Title.
SF375.P38   1985   636.3   84-21147
ISBN 0-396-08607-1

Contents

1 Springtime Lambs   9

2 Flocks of Sheep   25

3 Sheep for Wool   47

4 Breeds of Sheep   59

Index   80

· 1 ·

Springtime Lambs

Springtime is lamb time. Every spring day in roadside pastures, tiny new lambs appear beside their woolly mothers. Often, two or more babies are born to one mother sheep. When birth time comes, the mother sheep usually lies down on the ground. Muscles in her body help push her lamb or lambs into the world. The lamb's front legs normally come out first, followed by its head and the rest of its body. It is partly covered by a thin sac when it is born. The sac surrounded it while it grew inside its mother's body for five months. The sac almost always breaks open before the lamb is born. After her lamb is born, the female sheep, called a "ewe" (yoo), removes the remains of the sac with her mouth.

A lamb is born. If you look closely, you can see the head, front legs, and body inside the sac which surrounds the lamb.

A few moments after birth, the new lamb takes its first sputtering breath. The ewe licks her baby all over with her rough tongue, starting with its head. She also nibbles gently with her teeth as she licks. This dries the lamb off and stimulates its blood to flow, which helps it warm up faster.

The ewe on the right is "ma-a-a-ing" to her lamb so that the lamb will recognize its mother's voice.

At first the lamb is quiet. But soon it begins to
move. It shakes its head and jerks its legs. It makes its
first sound—a soft "ma-a-a-a." The mother sheep answers the baby with her own special low, throaty call.
From then on, the ewe and her baby will be able to recognize one another's voices. Soon the lamb gets its legs
under its body and struggles to its feet. At first, standing is difficult, and the lamb may fall down a few times.
But very quickly it can not only stand but also can walk
a few, awkward steps.

A newborn lamb is hungry. After standing, it nuzzles its mother, looking for her milk-filled udder. The udder is under the ewe's body, just in front of her hind legs. It has two fingerlike teats from which the lamb can suck the warm milk. The mother may nudge her lamb gently to help it find the milk. Soon the lamb is sucking away, drinking its first meal. The first milk which the mother's body makes for the lamb is very special. It contains chemicals made by her body which help protect the lamb from disease. If a lamb does not get this first milk, it can easily become sick and may die.

A ewe nurses her twins.

This black ewe has white triplets.

Most ewes make enough milk to feed twin lambs well. But often there is not enough to feed triplets. So when a ewe has three lambs, the owner often takes one of the lambs away. The extra lamb may be given to another ewe that has only one lamb or that has lost her own baby. It is not always easy to get a ewe to accept another mother's lamb. Each ewe knows how her own baby smells, so she can recognize a strange lamb. If a new mother cannot be found, the motherless "bum lamb" is kept in a protected place like a barn and fed from a bottle several times a day.

After they are a few days old, lambs with ewes caring for them can live in the barnyard or pasture. The ewes guard their babies as well as feeding them. While the lambs are little, the mother answers their every ma-a-a-a with her own call. This helps keep the lambs from getting lost. When a dog or a person comes into the pasture, the ewe stands in front of her lambs. She may give a warning "m-m-a-a-a" which says, "Stay away from my babies."

When a lamb nurses, it butts its head up against the ewe's udder. This helps make the milk flow freely. The lamb wiggles its long tail as it sucks. The lambs sometimes get down on their front knees to reach the low-hanging udder.

The ewe takes good care of her lambs. But they need some attention from humans, too. Their long tails need to be shortened. If an adult sheep had a long, woolly tail, it would get very dirty and heavy. So the owner puts a rubber band or special clip around the tail of each lamb. The band or clip cuts off the blood circulation to the tail, which dies and falls off. The lambs also get shots to protect them from sickness.

This boy and his lamb are friends.

When her lambs are taken away, the ewe bleats for them. She checks them over carefully when they are returned to make sure they are all right.

As the lambs grow older, they spend more and more time away from their mothers. They nibble at the grass. They join with one another and play. Lambs enjoy running and jumping together. They also play "king of the mountain" on hay bales and manure piles. Bit by bit, they become more independent from their mothers. They eat more and more grass and drink less and less milk. By the time they are a few months old, the lambs are on their own.

Lambs love to run and jump.

Children are proud of the lambs they raise when they take them to fairs.

Lambs are popular animals with children. Farm children often raise lambs to show in fairs. They take special care of these animals and hope to win prizes with them. The fairs are usually held in late summer, when the lambs are about six months old. The judges examine the animals carefully and give prizes to the best ones.

Sheep can thrive on poor pastures.

· 2 ·

Flocks of Sheep

Sheep are very useful animals. They provide people with tasty lamb to eat and with fine wool. Leather made from the skin of sheep makes soft gloves and other products. Sheepskins with the wool left on make cozy rugs and soft bed coverings for sick people. In some countries, sheep are raised for their milk as well as for meat and wool.

Sheep can thrive in poor pastures with little grass, where cows do not do well. Besides eating grass, sheep will get rid of many kinds of weeds that cows and horses leave alone. Sheep can even eat some plants which are poisonous to horses and cows without getting sick.

Sheep feed very differently than humans do. A sheep has no top teeth in the front of its mouth. Instead, the strong bottom teeth bite against a hard pad, which makes it easy to bite off clumps of tough grass. As the sheep grazes, it swallows the grass right away.

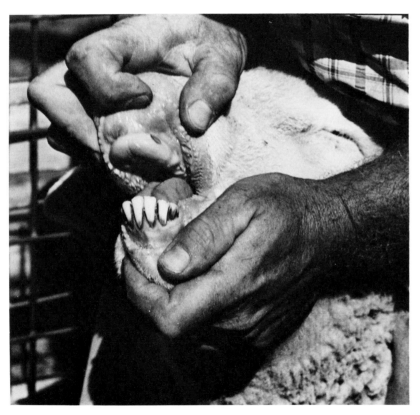

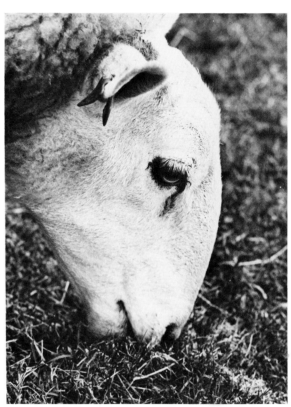

Here you can see the sheep's strong lower teeth and the upper pad against which they bite.

Sheep nip grass easily with their special mouths.

But later, while it is resting, it brings some of the food back into its mouth and chews it more thoroughly. Then it uses the big teeth in the back of its mouth to chew, grinding its teeth from side to side rather than chewing up and down the way we do.

This ewe is "chewing her cud," working on food which she swallowed and then brought back into her mouth for more chewing.

27

In America, sheep are raised on farms and ranches.
Sheep ranches own large numbers of sheep, often many
thousands. They graze on the range and receive little
attention from people for most of the year, except for
the lone shepherd who stays near them. Range sheep
are often pastured in the hills during the warm summer
and brought down into valleys closer to the ranch during the winter. When there are thousands of sheep, it
may take many days to move all of them from one area
to another. Range sheep are usually raised mainly for
their wool, although they are also sold for meat.

The sheep have a long way to go to their summer pasture.

In the fall, the lambs for market are separated from the flock.

In the fall, when the flocks are moved, the lambs to be sent to market are separated from the rest of the sheep. When the lambs are sold, they should weigh about one hundred pounds. One lamb of this size will produce about forty-five pounds of meat. In some countries, older sheep may also be sold for meat, called mutton.

The sheep are checked over for health in the fall, too.

The rams are kept separate from the ewes most of the year.

Their woolly coats protect sheep from the cold winds of winter.

Farm flocks have from a few sheep to five hundred or so. They are grazed on fenced pastures close to the farm. Farm flocks are sometimes raised mainly for meat and other times mostly for wool.

Most of the year, the male sheep, called rams, are kept separate from the ewes and lambs. But in the fall, rams are put in with the ewes for breeding. Only a few rams are needed, for each will mate with many ewes.

Sheep need special care during the winter and spring. They often need to be fed hay when the grass is not growing or snow is on the ground. In the spring-time, the ewes are brought in for lambing. After a ewe gives birth, she and her lamb or lambs are put into a small pen inside a warm barn. They stay there for only a few days. Then they are moved to a fenced pasture with a protected place to escape bad weather.

34

Even with no snow on the ground, sheep need to be fed in the winter when the grass is not growing.

Two rams run toward the hay wagon to be fed.

Then they eat their fill.

These ewes are waiting patiently for their lambs to be born.

The ewe and her new lamb are placed in a warm pen.

After a few days, the ewes and lambs are put back outdoors to live.

*The llama makes a good
sheep guard animal.*

Sheep, especially young lambs, are sometimes attacked by other animals. Coyotes, dogs, bears, foxes, and golden eagles are all able to kill and eat lambs. A shepherd travels among range sheep to keep an eye out for these predators—animals which kill sheep and eat them. Farm flocks may be brought indoors at night to protect them from predators.

Other animals, too, can be used to protect sheep from their enemies. The llama, an animal from South America which is related to camels, makes a good sheep guard. If a coyote or a dog comes near, the llama will chase it away.

A shepherd brings sheep down from the mountains in the fall. You can see his wagon, where he lives while out on the range, in the background.

The sheep, on the left, trusts the Komondor guard dog, on the right. The other dog is used for herding.

The Kuvasz is a fine guard dog.

Some kinds of dogs will protect sheep, too. The Great Pyrenees, Kuvasz, and Komondor are all big, white dogs used to guard sheep. When a puppy of one of these breeds is bought as a guard dog, it is raised with sheep. Then it will protect them when it grows up. A guard dog can even be left alone with the sheep on the range, as long as food is brought to it. If coyotes threaten, the guard dog will herd the sheep into a bunch and stand between them and the coyotes. Many farmers and ranchers with guard dogs lose no lambs at all to coyotes and other predators.

A Border Collie looks to her master for instructions.

Dogs are also used to help herd sheep. The herding breeds are very different from the guard ones. The Australian Shepherd and the Border Collie are both sheep herding breeds.

She swings wide and drives the sheep to the right.

These dogs can be trained to follow hand and voice signals. They can move sheep wherever the shepherd wants them taken and will retrieve any sheep which try to run away.

A new lamb has tiny tight curls of coarse wool on its body.

· 3 ·

Sheep for Wool

The ancestors of sheep raised today had long hair which was shed, like that of dogs or cats. When sheep were first tamed, they were probably raised for their meat and maybe for their milk. People also may have collected the long fibers when these early sheep shed and pounded them into felt. But somehow, sheep came along which did not lose their coats in the springtime. People figured out how to cut the wool off and make it into yarn.

These Merino sheep produce very fine wool.

When a lamb is born, it has small, tight curls of coarse wool. But as it grows, its wool grows, too. Just what the wool is like depends on the kind of sheep, for the wool varies greatly from one breed to the next. Most sheep have creamy white wool, but some are brown, black, or gray instead. Some breeds, such as the Navaho, have long, straight wool which is good for making carpets. Others, like the Merino, have very fine wool which makes soft sweaters and jackets.

Good wool has fine fibers with many tiny kinks in them. The finest wool has fibers which look like long, coiled springs. The coarsest wool has no kinks at all. You can tell a good wool sheep on a pasture by looking at it. It will look dirty, while a sheep with poor wool will look cleaner. This is because good, fine wool is so thick that dirt can't get through it. A thinner coat of coarse wool lets dirt in.

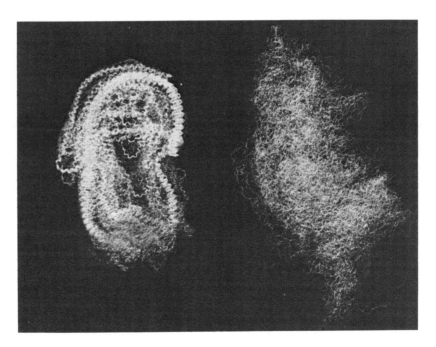

Merino wool, on the left, has many fine kinks in it. The wool from the Suffolk, a breed raised mainly for meat, is much coarser and lacks kinks.

Sheep have their long coats of wool cut off in the late spring or early summer. This is called shearing. Shearing sheep takes a great deal of skill. The men who do the job, called shearers, often travel from ranch to ranch. The shearer grabs the sheep and sits it on its rear end. The sheep usually does not struggle while it is being sheared. Shearers use electric clippers to remove the wool. They cut as close to the skin as possible so that the wool will be long. They do their best not to nick the sheep's skin.

The wool from one sheep is called a fleece. A fleece can weigh anywhere from about three pounds to over twenty pounds, depending on the size and breed of the sheep. Some wool is heavy because it has a lot of oil, called lanolin, in it. There can be several pounds of lanolin in an oily fleece. The lanolin is washed out of the wool and used to make hand lotion. Sheep shearers have soft hands from the lanolin in the wool.

Shearing sheep. The sheep on the left is getting a shot to protect it from disease, too.

A newly shorn sheep has lost its fluffy look.

When the sheep is sheared, the fleece is cut so that it all comes off as one piece. Then it is folded up and rolled so that the clean, inner wool is on the outside of the fleece. The fleece is tied and placed in a big bag along with the wool from other sheep.

At shearing time, the sheep are often given shots to protect them from diseases and may be run through a bath which helps heal skin diseases. Then they are set free, back out on the pasture.

The wool is packed into tall bags. The man is adding the last wool to a full bag.

Most wool is sold to companies that make it into yarn or weave it into cloth. But some people enjoy turning wool into clothing by hand. They buy the wool themselves, often directly from a sheep farmer. Sheep being raised for hand-spun wool must be carefully cared for. They need to be well fed at all times. If a sheep is poorly fed, or if it gets sick, the wool fibers will have weak places where they can break. The sheep must be kept as clean as possible so that burrs and hay do not get into the fleece.

Many hand spinners like to use fleeces with little lanolin so they can spin the wool without washing it first. Before the wool is turned into yarn, some spinners card the wool. Carding straightens the fibers, so they run in the same direction. It also helps remove dirt from the wool. When carding, the weaver combs the wool, using two flat wooden plates with metal teeth in them until it is smooth and straight.

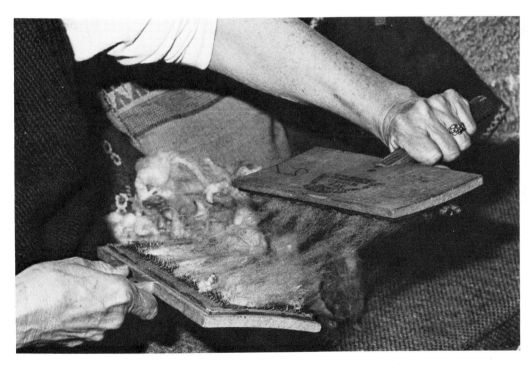

Wool is often carded to straighten the fibers and remove debris before spinning.

Wool yarn can be turned into beautiful warm clothing by knitting or crocheting it.

Then the wool is spun into yarn, using a spinning wheel. Most spinning wheels are turned by using a foot pedal. As the big wheel turns, it makes the small wheel in front of the spinner turn. The spinner holds the wool in her hands as it is gently pulled and twisted by the wheel. The newly made yarn is wound on a bobbin behind the small wheel. Later on, two strands of yarn are twisted together to make strong yarn. Then the yarn can be knitted or crocheted into clothing or woven into carpets.

On a spinning wheel, the foot pedal turns the big wheel, which turns the small wheel in front of the person operating the wheel. As the small wheel goes around, it gently twists the yarn, which is then wound onto a bobbin. You can see both white and black yarn on the bobbin in this photo.

Cross-bred lambs sometimes look a bit strange.

· 4 ·

Breeds of Sheep

Around the world, there are hundreds of breeds, or kinds, of sheep. Only some of these, however, are raised in America. Different sheep breeds are used for different purposes. Some breeds produce especially good meat. These sheep grow fast and put on a lot of muscle quickly. But their wool is not especially good. Other breeds grow long, fine coats of wool. But these sheep do not grow as fast as meat breeds, so their lambs are not as big or as meaty. Many sheep ranchers do not raise sheep of just one breed. They may cross one kind of ram with a different breed of ewe. The lambs which result will grow fairly quickly and have better wool than that of a pure-meat breed.

You can see that this flock contains more than one kind of sheep.

Dozens of sheep breeds are found in America. Most of these come from the British Isles. More than forty different breeds are found there.

The shortwool breeds are mostly hornless, usually with dark faces and legs. They have dense, somewhat coarse, wool and are raised mainly for their meat. These breeds usually do not stick together in flocks very well, so they are more difficult to herd than some other sheep.

Meat breed sheep vary in size. The Dorset ram behind is much bigger than the Suffolk ram in front. Suffolks are hornless, while some Dorsets have horns.

Suffolk

The Suffolk is a very familiar breed. Suffolks have
very dark faces and legs with no wool on them. Suffolks
and Suffolk crosses are popular for farm flocks.

The Hampshire is another popular breed for farms. These sheep are gentle and can live in different climates. Hampshires have dark noses, eyes, and ears. Some Hampshires have all dark faces, while others have a little light-colored wool between the eyes and nose. Hampshires are supposed to produce especially tasty lamb.

Hampshire

Southdown sheep have broad faces and small ears pointing outward. Their legs are short, and their faces are light. Southdowns are smaller than some other meat breeds, but their stocky bodies produce fine meat.

Southdown

An Oxford lamb

The Oxford is a big, hardy sheep with a brown face and stocky build. It is gentle and produces lots of white wool. Oxford wool is better than that of Hampshires and Suffolks.

The Dorset is different from other short-wooled breeds. It has a white face and white legs. Most Dorsets lack horns and are called "Polled Dorsets," but there are also Dorsets with horns. The Dorset is valuable because it can bear lambs at any time of year. A farmer in an area with a mild climate can have two lamb crops a year if he raises Dorsets.

Some other British breeds are called longwools. They have white faces and are usually hornless. These sheep have longer fleeces of coarser wool. Because the wool gets so long, some longwools need to be sheared twice a year.

The Border Leicester (LES- ter) has a long fleece, with no wool on its head or lower legs. These sheep are hardy and produce good meat.

Border Leicester

The Lincoln has long, curly, shiny wool. It is the biggest breed of sheep and is hardy and adaptable to different climates. Because its feet are strong, it does well in damp areas.

Lincoln

The Romney is another longwool breed which does well in damp climates. Like the Lincoln, the Romney has sound feet, and its thick fleece repels water. Romney wool is of better quality than that of other longwool breeds. Romneys are gentle and are easy to handle, which makes them good for farm flocks.

Scottish Blackface

In some parts of Great Britain, the sheep are left to themselves most of the year. These areas are often hilly, windy, and cold. Sheep breeds from the hill country are generally hardy, intelligent, and quick on their feet. Their lambs are strong and learn to stand and nurse quickly.

The Scottish Blackface is the most common breed found in Scotland and produces especially good meat. These handsome animals with sturdy horns are very hardy and independent minded. Their wool is unique. The fibers are coarse on the tips and downy underneath. This special coat allows the Blackface sheep to take very cold winters in stride.

The North Country Cheviot is an alert breed which can take good care of itself. These sheep will gather together when danger threatens, and ewes can discourage dogs and coyotes by stamping their feet and refusing to budge.

Wool sheep are raised in large numbers in Australia, New Zealand, and in the wide open spaces of the American West, as well as in farm flocks.

The best wool breeds do not come from Britain. The finest wool breed is the Merino, which came from Spain. The original Merinos had wrinkled skin, but most Merinos raised in America today have smooth skin and are called Delaine Merinos. These animals flock well together, so they are easy to control. Merino wool is the best there is, and each sheep produces a fleece weighing from twelve to over twenty pounds. Merinos are also used a great deal for crossbreeding.

The Rambouillet came from France, but it has been bred for a long time in America. This breed is especially adaptable to different climates and does well on the open range, even in the cold areas of the mountain west. The Rambouillet has fine wool and flocks well, so it is easy to control.

Rambouillet

A popular western breed is the Columbia. This hardy range sheep was developed early in this century in the United States by crossing Rambouillet ewes with Lincoln rams. The result is a hardy sheep with fairly good wool which grows quickly and forms flocks naturally.

The Corriedale was developed in Australia by crossing Merinos with longwool breeds, especially Lincolns. Corriedales have quite good wool but also grow fast and produce fine meat. They are gentle sheep which are easy to handle.

Karakul

Wool from many breeds, including Romneys, is popular with hand spinners. Hand spinners often like to use colored wool, and only five or six breeds raised in America, including the Lincoln and Merino, may produce colored fleeces.

The Karakul, from the area around Turkey, is often colored. Karakuls themselves have thin coats of coarse wool. But if they are crossed with other breeds, the resulting sheep have thicker, colored coats.

The American Navaho sheep, which may have four horns, has a long fleece which comes in many colors—black, gray, and different shades of brown. The wool from Navaho sheep is used to make beautiful hand-made rugs.

Navaho

The Jacob sheep is unusual. Not only does it often have four horns, it also has a coat with two or even three different colors. Jacob wool is very popular with hand spinners, who may separate out the colors or leave the wool as is.

78

Sheep are among the most useful animals raised by humans. They provide us with delicious meat and with wool to make beautiful clothing. In addition, they are interesting animals to learn about and appealing animals to look at, especially when they are young lambs.

Index

American Navaho sheep, 77
Australia, 71, 75
Australian Shepherd, 44

Birth, 9-11, 34
Border Collie, 44-45
Border Leister sheep, 67
Breeding, 33
Breeds of sheep, 48, 49, 59-78
British Isles, 60, 70
Bum lambs, 17

Carding wool, 55
Chewing, 27
Columbia sheep, 74
Corriedale sheep, 75
Cross-breeding, 58, 59, 72

Dorset sheep, 61, 66

Ewes, 9-23, 34, 39, 59

Fairs, 23
Farms flocks, 33, 62, 63, 69
Felt, 47
Fleece, 50, 52, 67
Food of sheep, 14, 18, 20, 24-27, 34-37
France, 73

Great Pyrenees 43

Guard dogs, 42-43

Hampshire sheep, 63, 65
Hand spinners, 54-56, 78
Herding dogs, 42, 44-45
Hill country breeds, 70
Horns, 61, 70

Jacob sheep, 78

Karakul sheep, 76
Komondor 42, 43
Kuvasz, 43

Lambs, 1, 2, 8, 9-23, 30, 34, 39, 46, 48, 85
Lanolin, 50, 55
Lincoln sheep, 68, 74, 75, 76
Llama, 40
Longwools, 67
Loom, 54

Meat, 28, 30, 33, 47, 59, 60, 63, 64, 67, 70, 75
Merino sheep, 48, 49, 72, 75, 76
Milk, 14, 17, 18, 47
Mutton, 30

North Country Cheviot sheep, 71

Oxford sheep, 65

Rambouillet sheep, 73, 74
Rams, 32, 33, 59, 61
Romney sheep, 69, 76

Scottish Blackface, 70
Shearing, 50-51
Sheep ranches, 28-31, 40, 41
Shepherd, 40, 41
Shortwools, 60
Shots, 51, 52
Sounds sheep make, 13, 18
Southdown sheep, 64
Spain, 72
Spinning wheel, 56-57
Suffolk sheep, 61, 62, 65

Triplets, 17
Turkey, 76

Udder, 14, 18

Winter, 34-37
Wool, 28, 33, 47-57, 59, 60, 67, 69, 70, 71, 73, 74, 75, 77, 78; colors of, 48, 76, 77, 78; quality of, 49

Yarn, 56